Our
Gift of Redemption

GOD'S PLAN TO SAVE THE WORLD

WRITTEN & ILLUSTRATED BY
LIZZIE DILLON

Our Gift of Redemption
GOD'S PLAN TO SAVE THE WORLD

New International Version (NIV)

Scripture quotations marked (NIV) are taken from the Holy Bible, New International Version®, NIV®. Copyright © 1973, 1978, 1984, 2011 by Biblica, Inc.™ Used by permission of Zondervan. All rights reserved worldwide. www.zondervan.com The "NIV" and "New International Version" are trademarks registered in the United States Patent and Trademark Office by Biblica, Inc.™

English Standard Version (ESV)

When noted (ESV) The Holy Bible, English Standard Version. ESV® Text Edition: 2016 Copyright © 2001 by Crossway, a publishing ministry of Good News Publishers. All rights reserved.

New King James Version (NKJV)

When noted (NKJV) scripture taken from the New King James Version®. Copyright © 1982 by Thomas Nelson. Used by permission. All rights reserved.

ISBN 978-1-937925-26-0 (Paperback)
Library of Congress Control Number: 2018947165

publishers
SOLUTION

Published in Southport, NC by Publishers Solution.
www.PublishersSolution.com

Cover, Interior Design & Illustrations by:

Megan Lizzie Dillon
Lizzie Dillon Artwork
lizziedillonartwork@gmail.com

Table of Contents

Introduction

*A*lways know... The Bible is **God's love letter** to us. It tells us that not only does He loves us, but also shows us what He has done to demonstrate that love. He has lovingly pursued us inspite of everything, so we could have a chance to spend eternity with Him. Never forget that the Bible is God's Word, given to us so we can know Him personally and follow Him daily.

2 Timothy 3:16 (NIV) says, *"All Scripture is breathed out by God and profitable for teaching, for reproof, for correction, and for training in righteousness, that the man of God may be complete, equipped for every good work."*

What is a Sinner's Heart?

Every human in the world is born with a sinner's heart. This means right from day one, each of us has what you would call "sin nature." What is sin you may ask? Sin means to "miss the mark." And what is that mark exactly? It is the standard of perfection that was established by God, our Creator. When we sin—disobey, lie, steal, hurt others, or even act selfishly—we do things our way, not God's.

Romans 3:23 (NIV) says, *"For all have sinned and fall short of the glory of God."* Not some, or most, but all.

Where Did Sin Come From?

"In the beginning, God created the heavens and the earth."
—Genesis 1:1 (NIV)

Soon after God created the heavens and the earth, He created mankind in His own image. From the dust, God formed man and breathed life into him to become a living being. He called him Adam. Moreover, He graciously gave man dominion over everything. God then commanded Adam that he may eat of any tree or plant in the garden except that of the Tree of the Knowledge of Good and Evil. He told him that if he were to eat from it, he would die.

Yet over time, God saw that Adam was lonely and needed a companion. So, He made the first woman from Adam's rib and called her Eve. Together they lived in the Garden of Eden.

Not long after, Satan entered into a serpent and tempted Eve. He told her that God knew if she were to eat of the Tree of the Knowledge of Good and Evil she would have the same knowledge as Him. Eventually, Eve gave in to the temptation and ate the forbidden fruit. Finding it so delicious she gave it to Adam. Once Adam ate from it, it changed humanity forever.

In time, God came to visit Adam and Eve in the Garden, but they hid as they realized their nakedness and tried to cover their bodies. When they revealed what they had done, God then gave Adam, Eve, and the serpent a punishment. For Adam, he would need to work the land and it would be a difficult task. For Eve, she would bear children with great pain. Lastly, for the serpent, he was to crawl on the ground and be more cursed than any other creature. Adam and Eve were then sent away from the Garden, and they were no longer able to talk to God face-to-face.

God knew He needed a plan to save mankind from their choice to sin, so they would have a chance of redemption and eternal life with Him.

The Lord God made garments of skin for Adam and [Eve] and clothed them. And the Lord God said, "The man has now become like one of us, knowing good and evil. He must not be allowed to reach out his hand and take also from the tree of life and eat, and live forever." So the Lord God banished him from the Garden of Eden to work the ground from which he had been taken. After He drove the man out, He placed on the east side of the Garden of Eden cherubim and a flaming sword flashing back and forth to guard the way to the tree of life.

GENESIS 3:21-24 (NIV)

The Birth of Jesus

nce sin was brought into the world, we as mankind were never the same again. It was not what God intended for us. But when God created us, He wanted us to have free will to choose—to *choose* to love Him. Not to be made to love Him. Unfortunately, in having the choice to choose, we chose wrong. This choice ultimately resulted in pain and death. So God had a plan that would save mankind from its own undoing. He decided to send His Son to earth to be born of a virgin mother.

Putting His plan in motion, God chose a young woman from Nazareth named Mary. Mary loved God very much and He knew she was the right woman for this blessing. She was also engaged to a carpenter named Joseph at the time.

One day the angel Gabriel came to Mary. She was startled but the angel continued to tell her, *"Do not be afraid, Mary; you have found favor with God. You will conceive and give birth to a Son, and you are to call Him Jesus. He will be great and will be called the Son of the Most High. The Lord*

God will give Him the throne of His father David, and He will reign over Jacob's descendants forever; His kingdom will never end." Luke 1:30-33 (NIV)

Mary wondered how this could be! The angel explained the Holy Spirit would come to her and the Holy Child would grow inside her. He would be called Emmanuel, which means "God is with us."

The angel then appeared to Joseph to let him know not to be afraid to take Mary as his wife. The baby who was conceived in her was from the Holy Spirit.

When the time came they traveled to Bethlehem and Mary gave birth to the Savior of the whole world. "And she gave birth to her firstborn Son and wrapped Him in swaddling cloths and laid Him in a manger, because there was no place for them in the inn." Luke 2:7 (ESV)

That night, an angel appeared in the sky to the shepherds in the field. They told of the Messiah that had been born to them that day. "And suddenly there was with the angel a multitude of the heavenly host praising God and saying,'Glory to God in the highest, and on earth peace among those with whom He is pleased!' When the angels went away from them into heaven, the shepherds said to one another, 'Let us go over to Bethlehem and see this thing that has happened, which the Lord has made known to us.'" Luke 2:13-15 (ESV)

So they hurried off and found Mary and Joseph, and the baby, who was lying in the manger. When they had seen Him, they spread the word concerning what had been told them about this Child, and all who heard it were amazed at what the shepherds said to them. But Mary treasured up all these things and pondered them in her heart. The shepherds returned, glorifying and praising God for all the things they had heard and seen, which were just as they had been told.

LUKE 2:16-20 (NIV)

The Followers of Jesus & His Miracles

"And Jesus grew in wisdom and stature,
and in favor with men and God."
—Luke 2:52 (NIV)

As Jesus matured and grew into a man, He began to start His ministry around the age of 30, which many of us have heard accounts of to this day. One of those events is when He went to the Jordan River to be baptized by John the Baptist, who was also His cousin. If you did not know, baptism is a sign of faith from a believer who has turned their life to God. Even though Jesus had never sinned, He wanted to show that He was rejecting the corruption that had entered the realm of Judaism—the religion among the Jewish people. Jesus wanted to be fully immersed in the values of the Kingdom of God that John was preaching to the crowd.

After His baptism, Jesus went into the wilderness to fast for 40 days and nights. It was here that He was tempted by Satan on multiple occasions. However, the devil eventually gave up and departed from Jesus as he could not persuade Him into temptation. Both His baptism and the temptation prepared Jesus to do the work God wanted Him to do. Now, Jesus was ready to start His mission and tell everyone that God had sent Him to save them from their sins for eternity. As He continued to preach, people began to follow Him. Along with them were 12 chosen disciples that Jesus had met along His travels— Simon Peter, Andrew, James (the son of Zebedee), John, Philip, Bartholomew, Thomas, Matthew, James (the son of Alphaeus), Thaddeus, Simon, and Judas Iscariot.

During His time with His disciples, Jesus did many miracles. To casting out demons, healing the sick, turning water into wine, feeding a crowd of 5,000 people with only two fish and five loaves of bread, and even walking on water while calming the stormy seas. And all the while, Jesus continued to preach the Good News wherever He went.

"Come," He said. Then Peter got down out of the boat, walked on the water and came toward Jesus. But when he saw the wind, he was afraid and, beginning to sink, cried out, "Lord, save me!" Immediately Jesus reached out His hand and caught him. "You of little faith," He said, "why did you doubt?" And when they climbed into the boat, the wind died down. Then those who were in the boat worshiped Him, saying, "Truly you are the Son of God."

MATTHEW 14:29-33 (NIV)

The Crucifixion of Jesus

Though Jesus was spreading the Good News and doing many wonderful miracles, not everyone was happy about the situation. On numerous occasions, Jesus angered religious men known then as the Pharisees. These men were seeking any way to get rid of Him as Jesus would call them out for their prideful and sinful ways. So, they patiently waited for their chance to dispose of Him.

One day, Jesus told His disciples that soon He would no longer be with them as He would be betrayed by one of them. It saddened the disciples very much as they wondered which one of them could do such a thing to their Lord and Master. However, He told them that He was going to prepare a place for them where they would spend eternity with Him.

Not long after, Jesus went to the Garden of Gethsemane to pray with some of His disciples. He knew the time was near. It was then that He was betrayed by Judas Iscariot and arrested by city officials sent by the Pharisees. Jesus was quickly put on trial with Pilate, the governor of Rome. While Pilate was presiding over the proceedings, Jesus was beaten and tortured severely. The soldiers also placed a crown of thorns on His head and clothed Him in a purple robe to mock Him. They yelled, "Hail, King of the Jews!" while they continued to whip and beat Him. Afterwards, the soldiers brought Him back before Pilate so he could display Jesus to the crowd. However, they were not satisfied and cried, "Crucify Him!" Pilate relented and gave Jesus over to the mob.

Jesus carried His own cross up to Golgotha where they crucified Him with two thieves on either side. They hung a sign above Him that read: "Jesus of Nazareth, The King of the Jews." *"Near the cross of Jesus stood His mother, His mother's sister, Mary the wife of Clopas, and Mary Magdalene. When Jesus saw His mother there, and the disciple whom He loved standing nearby, He said to her, 'Woman, here is your son,' and to the disciple, 'Here is your mother.' From that time on, this disciple took her into his home."* John 19: 25-27 (NIV)

Jesus was in excruciating pain on the cross not only because of the pain of such a death, but because He was bearing the weight of all of mankind's sin on His back. Can you imagine someone loving you that much that they would choose to do this for you? Take a moment to let that sink in. Even if it had only been *just you,* Jesus would have gone to the cross even for just one single soul. That is true love.

And when Jesus had cried out again in a loud voice, he gave up His spirit. At that moment the curtain of the temple was torn in two from top to bottom. The earth shook, the rocks split and the tombs broke open. The bodies of many holy people who had died were raised to life. When the centurion and those with Him who were guarding Jesus saw the earthquake and all that had happened, they were terrified, and exclaimed, "Surely He was the Son of God!"

MATTHEW 27:50-52,54 (NIV)

The Burial & Resurrection of Jesus

After Jesus' crucifixion a man named Joseph of Arimathea asked Pilate for the body of Jesus. Pilate gave his permission, so Joseph took His body away. With the help of Joseph's friend, Nicodemus, they took Jesus' body and wrapped it with spices in strips of linen in accordance with Jewish burial customs. They laid His body to rest in a tomb belonging to Joseph in a garden near where Jesus was crucified.

During this time, the Sabbath had finished, and the morning of the first day of the week had come. Early that morning, Mary Magdalene and Mary visited the tomb and saw that the stone sealing the tomb had been rolled away. *"And behold, there was a great earthquake, for an angel of the Lord descended from heaven and came and rolled back the stone and sat on it... But the angel said to the women, 'Do not be afraid, for I know that you seek*

Jesus who was crucified. He is not here, for He has risen, as He said. Come, see the place where He lay. Then go quickly and tell His disciples that He has risen from the dead, and behold, He is going before you to Galilee; there you will see Him. See, I have told you.' So they departed quickly from the tomb with fear and great joy, and ran to tell His disciples." Matthew 28:2, 5-8 (NIV)

When the women reported what they had seen to the disciples, they did not believe it. They decided to go to the tomb to see for themselves. Once they saw that the women were indeed correct, they did not understand what had happened. Where had Jesus gone?!

They eventually resigned themselves to the situation as what could they do after all? So they went back to where they were staying. However, it was not long before Jesus appeared to His disciples. He then showed them His nail-marked hands to convince them He was truly their Lord and Savior. There was no doubting after that—it was Jesus, and He was alive!

Now Thomas, one of the Twelve, was not with the disciples when Jesus came. So the other disciples told him, "We have seen the Lord!" But he said to them, "Unless I see the nail marks in His hands and put my finger where the nails were, and put my hand into His side, I will not believe." A week later His disciples were in the house again, and Thomas was with them. Though the doors were locked, Jesus came and stood among them and said, "Peace be with you!" Then He said to Thomas, "Put your finger here; see My hands. Reach out your hand and put it into My side. Stop doubting and believe." Thomas said to Him, "My Lord and my God!" Then Jesus told him, "Because you have seen Me, you have believed; blessed are those who have not seen and yet have believed."

JOHN 20:24-29 (NIV)

The Ascension of Jesus

*J*esus appeared to the disciples for another 40 days after His resurrection. He wanted to make sure they knew He was surely alive!

In their encounters, Jesus spoke to them of the Kingdom of God and explained to them about the prophecies He had fulfilled so they could be confident that He was the Messiah.

During Jesus' final moments with the disciples He made them a promise that the Holy Spirit would come upon them. *"But the Advocate, the Holy Spirit, whom the Father will send in my name, will teach you all things and will remind you of everything I have said to you. Peace I leave with you; my peace I give you. I do not give to you as the world gives. Do not let your hearts be troubled and do not be afraid."* John 14:26-27 (NIV)

He then commanded them as followers of Christ to preach the Gospel: *"But you will receive power when the Holy Spirit comes on you; and you will be My witnesses in*

Jerusalem, and in all Judea and Samaria, and to the ends of the earth." Acts 1:8 (NIV)

"Therefore go and make disciples of all nations, baptizing them in the name of the Father and of the Son and of the Holy Spirit, and teaching them to obey everything I have commanded you. And surely I am with you always, to the very end of the age." Matthew 28:19-20 (NIV)

Jesus wanted the disciples to tell the story of how He came to earth, died on the cross for our sins, was buried and raised from the dead on the third day. They were to make followers of Christ, so that they may tell the Good News.

Shortly after this, Jesus' feet lifted off the ground. He ascended into the sky toward Heaven, where He went to reside and sit down at the right hand of God, just waiting to come back one day for His bride—the Church.

After He said this, He was taken up before their very eyes, and a cloud hid Him from their sight. They were looking intently up into the sky as He was going, when suddenly two men dressed in white stood beside them. "Men of Galilee," they said, "why do you stand here looking into the sky? This same Jesus, who has been taken from you into heaven, will come back in the same way you have seen Him go into heaven." Then the apostles returned to Jerusalem from the hill called the Mount of Olives, a Sabbath day's walk from the city.

ACTS 1:9-12 (NIV)

How to Be Saved by God's Grace

Can you believe that God did all that just to save us? He sent His Son down to earth so we could be spared from an eternity in Hell apart from Him. He gave us an escape route. We just have to accept Him as Lord and Savior of our lives and let the Holy Spirit guide us to live for Christ and share His glorious story.

How can we do this?

1. We have to know that Jesus is the only way to Heaven. Apart from God we cannot earn our way into Heaven by good works or even with good intentions.

    "Nor is there salvation in any other, for there is no other name under Heaven given among men by which we must be saved." Acts 4:12 (NKJV) *"...I am the way and the truth and the life. No one comes to the Father except through me."* John 14:6 (NIV)

2. We must acknowledge we are sinners and ask for forgiveness of our sins.

    "If we confess our sins, He is faithful and just to forgive us our sins and to cleanse us from all unrighteousness." 1 John 1:9 (ESV)

3. We must acknowledge and trust that Jesus is Lord and Savior of our lives.

    "If you declare with your mouth, 'Jesus is Lord,' and believe in your heart that God raised Him from the dead, you will be saved." Romans 10:9 (NIV)

4. We must ask Him to come into our lives and have full reign over it. He wants our willing surrender to Him. We must allow Christ to work and fulfill His purpose through us and hand our lives over to Him.

    For we know that one day, *that at the name of Jesus every knee should bow, in heaven and on earth and under the earth, and every tongue acknowledge that Jesus Christ is Lord, to the glory of God the Father."* Philippians 2:10-11 (NIV)

This must be a sincere change in our heart to truly be saved. Understand the weight of this decision you are making and be sure you understand what it means to be saved. If you have any questions, find a pastor or someone you know who believes the Bible who can help you in your spiritual journey. When you are ready, God will be waiting with the open arms of a loving Father to accept you into His family.

The fact that
our heart yearns
for something
Earth can't supply
is proof that Heaven
must be our home.

C. S. LEWIS

The deepest longing
of the human heart
is to know and enjoy
the glory of God. We
were made for this.

JOHN PIPER

Show the World Your Faith

Once a person has made the decision to become a follower of Christ, their life should be a light to the world. A light that cannot be ignored by any that are around it. Our lives should be like a stone thrown in a pond. If you have ever done this or seen it, you know that ripples start to go out from where the stone hits the water and it continues to grow. This is a beautiful illustration of how our faith should spread to others.

"And this gospel of the kingdom will be preached in the whole world as a testimony to all nations, and then the end will come." Matthew 24:14 (NIV)

As followers of Christ, just as Jesus told His disciples to go and make disciples of all nations, so should we do so today. When you are a Christian, you are commanded by the Lord Himself to take the Good News to all the world until the end of ages when Jesus will return for us. We need to be sharing and praying for those that need Jesus. But how can one contain this news and not tell their friends and family?! Every day we should be sharing our own story of redemption and how it changed our life and, of course, the story of God's redemption for us all.

Put Words Into { A C T I O N }

We should tell the world of our life-changing decision for Christ and a way of professing that is through baptism. This act of faith shows your old ways have fallen away, and you have been cleansed by the blood of the Lamb. Go talk to a pastor today about being baptized as a profession of your faith in Jesus Christ!

Catch on fire with enthusiasm and people
will come for miles to watch you burn.

CHARLES WESLEY

The only way the Body of Christ will
fulfill the mission Christ has given it is
for individual Christians to have a vision
for fulfilling that mission personally.

DAVID JEREMIAH

To be a soul winner is the happiest thing
in this world. And with every soul you
bring to Jesus Christ, you seem to get a
new heaven here upon earth.

CHARLES SPURGEON

One Day We Will Be Home

"And if I go and prepare a place for you,
I will come back and take you to be with me
that you also may be where I am."
—John 14:3 (NIV)

This world is not for long. There will come a time of great tribulation and sadness after the Rapture of the church, an event when all Christian believers—living and dead—will rise and join Christ in the sky. But once that time has passed Jesus Himself has promised us a place where there will be "no more tears or death." There will come a New Heaven and a New Earth. It will be the Garden of Eden restored, but even better than before. We as humans can only anticipate what else God has in store for us for all of eternity.

"And I saw no temple in the city, for its temple is the Lord God the Almighty and the Lamb. And the city has no need of sun or moon to shine on it, for the glory of God gives it light, and its lamp is the Lamb. By its light will the nations walk, and the kings of the earth will bring their glory into it, and its gates will never be shut by day—and there will

be no night there. They will bring into it the glory and the honor of the nations. But nothing unclean will ever enter it, nor anyone who does what is detestable or false, but only those who are written in the Lamb's Book of Life."
Revelation 21:22-27 (ESV)

Sinner's Prayer

"And everyone who calls
on the name of the Lord will be saved."
—Acts 2:21 (NIV)

I f you do not have a personal relationship with Jesus Christ today I prayerfully challenge you to consider praying this prayer to accept Him as your Lord and Savior. The time draws near when He is coming back for His bride…His church…His people.

Dear Heavenly Father, I come to you in prayer asking for the forgiveness of my sins. I confess with my mouth and believe with my heart that Jesus is Your Son, and that He died on the cross that I might be forgiven and have eternal life through Him. Father, I believe that Jesus rose from the dead and I ask you right now to come into my life and be my personal Lord and Savior. I repent of my sins. I will follow and worship you all of my days because your Word is truth. I confess that I am a born again believer cleansed by the blood of the Lamb—Jesus Christ! In Jesus' Name, Amen!

Remember Your Spiritual Birthday

D on't ever forget the day that you made the decision to turn your heart and life over to Jesus Christ. What a wonderful decision that you have made! Proclaim to the world your faith. Write in your name, the date you made your decision, and sign it.

Today I made the decision to turn my heart and life over to Jesus Christ. Let me remember to always celebrate this wonderful gift of redemption that has been made available to me through the sacrifice of God's Son.

Name: _____

Date: _____

Signature: _____

From One Awakened Heart to Another

I n February 2015, I was sitting in a church utterly devastated and broken. My life was falling apart in so many ways. I did not even know where to begin. As tears were rolling down my face during the pastor's sermon God laid it on my heart that I needed to use my talent of art to serve Him by telling the story of His love and redemption. I had never had something so clearly put on my heart from the Holy Spirit so I knew it was an important calling.

Through many ups and downs of life it took over three years to finish this mission. But I knew that even when it was hard and Satan would attack me when I would make progress on the book it would be worth it. If Satan was attacking then God's glory was definitely going to abound in it and His will and work would be done.

To those of you that read this book and received salvation, you are the reason for this book. You are the reason for it all. I welcome you into God's family, my precious brothers and sisters. I cannot wait to meet you one day in our heavenly home where we will all live for eternity with God our Father. Please share the good news with others and spread it like wild fire. Let our hearts burn for Him!

To those using this as a tool to reach others, thank you for being apart of this command we have all been given and by helping to make this God-given venture ripple into an even bigger effect then I will ever be able to imagine. I know God will do great things and open doors for people to be reached with it.

Please be in prayer for this endeavor as it is used to reach others and as it is prayerfully translated from English into many other languages.

Thank you for being apart of this journey!

Lizzie Dillon

A Verse of Encouragement

As I went through some of my darkest days I was given a verse by the man who is now my husband. He saw the pain, the trials, the fear and the hurt I was going through. I had never had a life verse, but from the moment he read it to encourage me it became mine. Now I want to share it with you. No matter if you are going through a difficult situation, you are on the mission field, or you just need to know God is with you *"wherever you go,"* remember these words with your whole mind and your whole heart.

"Have I not commanded you? Be strong and courageous.
Do not be afraid; do not be discouraged, for the Lord
your God will be with you wherever you go."

—Joshua 1:9 (NIV)

Notes

www.ingramcontent.com/pod-product-compliance
Lightning Source LLC
Chambersburg PA
CBHW040616060426
42445CB00039B/1979